The Bridges of Madison County Memory Book

The
BRIDGES
of
MADISON
COUNTY
Memory Book

With photographs by
CLINT EASTWOOD

WARNER BOOKS

A Time Warner Company

Warner Books, Inc., 1271 Avenue of the Americas, New York, NY 10020

 A Time Warner Company

Printed in Mexico.
First Printing: June 1995
10 9 8 7 6 5 4 3 2 1

LC: 95-60627
ISBN: 0-446-51998-7

Credits

. . . come near me, while I sing the ancient ways . . . William Butler Yeats

. . . I have spread my dreams under your feet . . . William Butler Yeats

. . . I swayed my leaves and flowers in the sun . . . William Butler Yeats

. . . I hear it in the deep heart's core . . . William Butler Yeats

. . . we have been moving toward each other all our lives . . . Robert James Waller, *The Bridges of Madison County*

. . . I'll wonder for the rest of my life what happened here . . . Richard Lagravenese, Screenwriter, *The Bridges of Madison County*, the film

. . . each to see the other whole against the sky . . . Rainer Maria Rilke

. . . I look through the lens, and you're there . . . Robert James Waller, *The Bridges of Madison County*

. . . carry the sun in a golden cup . . . William Butler Yeats

. . . the only thing I've done was to make my way to you . . . Robert James Waller, *The Bridges of Madison County*

. . . we long to tread a way none trod before . . . William Butler Yeats

. . . such certainty comes only once and never again . . . Robert James Waller, *The Bridges of Madison County*

. . . you never think that love like this can happen to you . . . Richard Lagravenese, Screenwriter, *The Bridges of Madison County*, the film

. . . no matter how many lifetimes you live . . . Richard Lagravenese, Screenwriter, *The Bridges of Madison County*, the film

. . . maybe we'll accidentally run into each other . . . Richard Lagravenese, Screenwriter, *The Bridges of Madison County*, the film

. . . we were bound together as tightly as two people can be . . . Richard Lagravenese, Screenwriter, *The Bridges of Madison County*, the film

. . . I can't say goodbye yet . . . Richard Lagravenese, Screenwriter, *The Bridges of Madison County*, the film

. . . to ancient evenings and distant music . . . Robert James Waller, *The Bridges of Madison County*

Dear Marty,

    I just saw this little book
& liked it. I know it's probably
for lovers, but I mean it as
a loving friend.

    After all a friend is a friend
is a friend - - - -

                Love,
                  Judy

...come near me, while I sing the ancient ways...

... I have spread my dreams
under your feet...

...I swayed my leaves and flowers
in the sun...

...I hear it in the deep
heart's core...

...we have been moving toward
each other all our lives...

...I'll wonder for the rest of my
life what happened here...

... each to see the other
whole against the sky...

... I look through the
lens, and you're there...

... carry the sun in a
golden cup...

...the only thing I've done
was to make my way to you...

...we long to tread a way none trod before...

...such certainty comes
only once and never again...

... you never think that love like this can happen to you...

...no matter how many
lifetimes you live...

...maybe we'll accidentally run
into each other...

...I can't say goodbye yet...

... we were bound together as tightly as two people can be...

...to ancient evenings and
distant music...